UNDER THE WINGS OF THE ALMIGHTY

Sermons For Pentecost (Last Third)
Cycle A First Lesson Texts

BY ROBERT F. SIMS

C.S.S. Publishing Co., Inc.
Lima, Ohio

Library of Congress Cataloging-in-Publication Data

Sims, Robert F., 1936-
 Under the wings of the Almighty : sermons for Pentecost (last third) Cycle A First Lesson texts / by Robert F. Simms
  p.   cm.
 ISBN 1-55673-432-8
 1. Pentecost season — Sermons.   2. Sermons, American.   3. Lutheran Church — Sermons.   I. Title.
BV4300.5.S55   1992
252'.6—dc20   92-6282
                                                   CIP

9235 / ISBN 1-55673-432-8   PRINTED IN U.S.A.

■————————————————————————■

This book is dedicated to my parents,
Mr. and Mrs. Joe L. Sims, in grateful ap-
preciation for a lifetime of support and
encouragement.

■————————————————————————■

Table Of Contents

Foreword

Dr. Robert F. Sims, senior pastor of the Lutheran Church of the Redeemer on famous Peachtree Street in Atlanta, speaks from a pulpit that in turn speaks to both pulpiteer and people. Redeemer's pulpit was designed to express a theology of preaching. A pulpit definitely influences the style and message of the preacher. The influence can be seen in this collection of sermons.

The location of a pulpit says something about the place of preaching in a church's life. Redeemer's pulpit is not centrally located in the chancel as if to say that preaching is the sole reason for coming to church. Rather, it is located on the gospel side of the church to indicate that the sermon is a sacramental act of worship. The sacrament is the Word, which brings grace when it is proclaimed. This calls for liturgical preaching based upon the lectionary and liturgy. The sermons of Dr. Sims are based upon the first lesson for the final third of the Pentecost season.

How is the Word, taken from the lectionary, to be interpreted? Redeemer's pulpit has a top border of wood carvings depicting the major events in the life of Martin Luther. In other words, this is a Lutheran pulpit and the person in the pulpit is to emulate Luther in boldly declaring the Word. To do so demands biblical preaching, for the characteristic portrayal of Luther in stained glass, statuary, and painting is Luther dressed in a clerical robe pointing his finger to a passage in an open Bible. Luther said, "Preaching is the Word of God." Preaching is the Word of God when the Word is preached. Readers of this book of sermons will find that the theme of the sermons is taken from the text and beautifully and helpfully related to life today. And these texts, except for one, are from the Old Testament! Who says the Old Testament cannot speak to modern society and still be true to God's revelation in Christ?

Speaking of biblical preaching, Redeemer's pulpit has a desk just large enough for a big Bible evident to the worshipers. The purpose of this is to enable the preacher entering the pulpit to turn the pages of the Bible to the text of the sermon. The congregation sees that the sermon will be coming from God's Word. The desk was purposely made small to leave no room for a sermon manuscript or notes. It calls for the preacher to communicate directly, eye to eye, heart to heart as the most effective means of communication. A paper curtain is not to separate the people from the preacher.

Redeemer's pulpit calls for biblical preaching, but what is that? The answer is found on the pillar next to the pulpit. Carved into the limestone are the words seen only by the preacher entering the pulpit: "Sir, we would see Jesus (John 12:21)." This is the people's plea to the preacher. They want to see Jesus, for he is the incarnate Word of God, the heart and center of the Bible, and the final and perfect revelation of God, full of grace and truth. Paul had the same conviction: "For what we preach is not ourselves but Jesus Christ as Lord (2 Corinthians 4:5)." Accordingly, Dr. Sims' sermons in this collection are Christocentric and Jesus is exalted as Lord and Savior.

Who or what or where is the source of a preacher's insight and power? What makes for dynamic preaching? Redeemer's pulpit points to the Holy Spirit. He is represented by a red dove fastened to the ceiling of the pulpit tester. It happens to hang just above the preacher's head when in the pulpit. Christian preaching began on Pentecost when the Spirit came to the Apostles. Luke reports that they "began to speak in other tongues as the Spirit gave them utterance (Acts 2:4)." What makes a sermon come alive? The Spirit! What fills the preacher with enthusiasm? Again, the Spirit! Without the Spirit a sermon is deadly dull and lifeless. A reading of Dr. Sims' sermons reveals that the Spirit possessed him as he prepared these sermons. They are full of compassion and pastoral concern. According to Paul, the first fruit of the Spirit is love (Galatians 5:22)."

Redeemer's pulpit speaks not only to the preacher but also to the people. On the front of the pulpit in beautifully carved letters is Jeremiah's cry to his people: "O earth, earth, earth, hear the word of the Lord (Jeremiah 22:29)." Hearing God's Word leads to life and salvation. Paul declares, "So faith comes from what is heard, and what is heard comes by the preaching of Christ (Romans 10:17)." Hear the preacher's appeal — repent and believe! O my people, why will you die? O hear the truth, for God's Word is truth! Throughout these nine sermons in the book we hear a prophet like Jeremiah calling, crying, beseeching, pleading with people to hear God's Word that they might have life today and for eternity.

I am convinced that Redeemer's pulpit has had a beneficial effect upon Dr. Sims' preaching. In reading these sermons I felt a pastor's love for his people. Profusely illustrated, the sermons are interesting and contemporary. The subjects of the sermons deal with pressing personal and social problems with the solution always found in repentance and faith in Christ. My soul was fed by these sermons, and I am sure they will feed the souls of other readers as well.

— John R. Brokhoff

The Call To Excellence

The time had come for Moses to be "gathered to his people as his brother Aaron was gathered (Numbers 27:13)." Moses, knowing that the people could not go on without the one who would lead, prayed to God: "Appoint a man over the congregation . . . who shall lead them out and bring them in; that the congregation of the Lord shall not be as sheep who have no shepherd (Numbers 27:16-17)." God heard the prayer of Moses and appointed Joshua, "A man in whom is the spirit (Numbers 27:18)."

Throughout the centuries God has appointed shepherds for his people. Some were determined dynamic leaders like Joshua. Others were fiery prophets like Elijah. Some were gentle spirits like John. Like Joshua, all were ordained to lead God's people into the promised land of tomorrow.

The question before the church today is what kind of pastors must we have to lead the church into the future? Listen to the answer given in this poem.

> *Give me a man of God, one man whose faith is master*
> *of his mind,*
> *and I will right all wrongs and bless the name of*
> *all mankind.*

Give me a man of God, one man whose tongue is touched
     with heaven's fire
and I will flame the darkest hearts with high resolve
     and clear desire.

Give me a man of God, one man, one mighty prophet
     of the Lord,
and I will give you peace on earth bought with a
     prayer and not a sword.

Give me a man of God, one man true to the vision that
     he sees,
and I will build your broken shrines and bring the
     nations to their knees.
George Liddell

Do you hear what is being asked of today's ministers of the gospel? Do you hear what's needed for the future? Excellence is what is needed; excellence in faith and commitment. Pastors are asked to give their best to God without excuse, without complaint or compromise, their best for God.

Many writers are telling us about the empty pulpit. We are told that by the year 2000 many pastors of the church will reach retirement age and there will not be sufficient numbers to take their places. The implication is that we need more and more pastors. Even though I appreciate the problem the church is facing in the future, I firmly believe that what the church needs today is not more and more pastors but better and better pastors. We need pastors who are far more concerned about building their congregations than their careers; pastors who are more concerned about glorifying God than themselves; pastors who are willing to work 60 hours a week and count it the least they can do for the One who has done everything for them.

We've heard much lately about "burnout" among the clergy. I am sympathetic, and understand why the burnout happens. I know pastors who have been overworked and overstressed. Under the pressure they have burned out and many have dropped out. However, let me be honest with you and say that I am far less concerned about burnout among clergy than I am about cop out. I know far more ministers who are giving too little to the church than those who are giving too much. I am far less concerned about pastors being overworked as I am about their being under-committed. I know too many pastors who are far more concerned about their days off than their days on; more concerned about their vacation than their dedication.

So what's happening in the seminaries today? I believe the training is good. I believe it is better than it was 25 years ago. I believe there are few pastors who are truly inept and inadequate. At the same time I believe that there are few pastors who are truly extraordinary and exceptional who can assume leadership not only for their congregations but for their communities. In recent years we have pulled in from both extremes. There are fewer poor pastors and fewer good ones. We have, as a result, created a majority of mediocrity. I do not believe that mediocrity will serve the demands of the life of the church of the future. I hear too many pastors who are concerned about security with their jobs rather than service in their church. I hear too many pastors who are willing to promote the appearance of piety and the illusion of progress in order to maintain what they have. When one looks beneath the surface, one discovers that the piety has no depth; that the progress is not real. In fact, across the last 20 years, mainline churches in this country have lost 20 percent of their total membership.

I hear far too much concern about security. In a recent meeting with pastors the conversation around the table was about burnout among clergy. The pastors conducted an impromptu poll measuring on a scale of one to 10 (10 being high) their level of stress. One pastor volunteered, "My stress level is rather high, about seven or eight on that scale." Others indicated, however, that their stress was rather low, perhaps four or five at the highest. "The truth is," said one pastor, "I'm pretty comfortable where I am. In fact, I've learned that as long as I don't steal the church's money or run off with the church's secretary, I'm pretty secure." Inherent in the comment was an obvious concern for security. I did not realize that security was the basic issue in ministry.

All of these years I've labored under the illusion that ministry has something to do with service to the church. I find it hard to imagine the apostle Paul searching for security as he went from jail to prison to beating to stoning to shipwreck and to prison again. I cannot imagine that Simon Peter was worried much about security when he left Palestine to go to Rome to work with the church under the persecutions of Nero. I find it difficult to imagine Martin Luther being overly concerned about security as he stood before Charles V, the emperor of the Holy Roman Empire and said, "I cannot, I will not recant. God help me. Here I stand."

I can't help but wonder, where are the mighty prophets with fire in their souls? Where are the men and women with vision who will shepherd the flock, who will lead the people of God into the future?

Where are the lay people who will demand excellence by giving excellence? Through our baptism we are all ordained into the ministry of the Word of God. Some of us go to seminary and are trained for special tasks in the church. Others are lay ministers and carry out the assignment of protecting the purity of the gospel and proclaiming the Word in daily life. We are all ministers of the gospel; and the people in the pew, the lay ministers of the church, have the right to demand excellence only if they give excellence. Excellence is required in your worship attendance, in your study of the Word and in your attendance to prayer. Excellence is required in your stewardship, the giving of your resources and in making yourself available for service in the church. Excellence is the issue. Lay members have a right to expect it and to demand it if they give it. I assure you the future will require it.

You understand, don't you, the importance of excellence among those shepherds who will lead the people? The church has an awesome assignment for the future. We are called to carry the redemptive process to the world of tomorrow. We cannot do that with a mediocre ministry. The major changes that have taken place in the world in recent years did not happen because the church of Christ was there to champion the cause of the cross. The church has been so preoccupied with making people feel good that it has lost the power to inspire people to do good. The Berlin Wall did not fall and crumble because those people saw the great example of our Christian faith and decided that they, too, wanted to have a Christian society. No, they looked at the Western world and decided they wanted a capitalistic society. Communism is not failing today because the people of Russia have looked to the West and decided that they want to have a Christian way of life. They've looked to the West and decided they want to have a consumer's way of life. The Viet Nam War did not end because the church of Christ stood up in righteous indignation and said we will not tolerate it. It came to an end because politicians stood up and said, "We will not pay for it."

The important changes that have happened in recent years did not happen because of the influence of the church. The battle that is being fought today for the rights of abused children and battered women is not being fought by pastors and people in churches. That battle is being waged by lawyers in courtrooms. The world cries out for peace of mind but that cry is not being answered by theologians offering new and different ways of worship and meditation. That cry is being answered by psychiatrists who are offering new and different forms of medication.

Do you understand that the church is not having the impact it should in the world? I ask, where are the prophets with fire in their souls and the men and women of vision who will shepherd the flock and lead the people?

Jesus said in John's gospel, "I am the Good Shepherd. I know my own and my own know me and they listen to my voice." I ask you, friends, what voice is the world listening to today? Is the world listening to the voice of Christ as he speaks through his ministers? Are we content for the world of tomorrow to be shaped by the voices of politicians, economists, advertisers or consumers?

The issue for the church of tomorrow is not quantity, friends, it's quality. What the church needs today is not more and more but better and better. The issue is excellence; the issue is always excellence in the church. We are called upon to give our best.

Today let us make a commitment in our minds and hearts, since we are the ministers of the gospel, that we will aspire to excellence and that we will, in this place and at this time, give our best to God. Amen.

Whether We Live Or Die

"So Moses, a servant of the Lord, died there in the land of Moab (Deuteronomy 34:5)."

In life and in death, Moses was a servant of God. The issue for Moses was not to live or to die but in all things to belong to God. The apostle Paul reflects the same spirit, "None of us lives to himself and none of us dies to himself. If we live we live to the Lord and if we die, we die to the Lord. So whether we live or whether we die, we are the Lord's (Romans 14:7-8)." All who trust and believe in God belong to God. We recognize that life is his treasured gift and comes to us by his grace. We are the Lord's. Whether we live or whether we die, we are the Lord's. These words heal and comfort in times when we need healing and comfort in a desperate way.

A man committed suicide. He was a good man. He was 62 years old, strong, energetic and successful. He had an excellent law practice and was a long-time member of his church council. He had a great personality and a wonderful sense of humor. On a Wednesday morning he climbed on the elevator in his office building. A young woman who worked there stepped on with him. She asked, "Are you going up?" "No," he replied, "I'm going down but I'm in no hurry today. We'll go up first." She stepped off at the second floor, smiled and said, "Have a good day." He answered, "Oh, I always try to have a good day." The elevator doors closed. He went down to the basement, stepped off, went into a room, closed the door, lay down on the floor and put a bullet in his head.

I sat in the funeral in solemn silence, barely hearing the droning words of the preacher. Deep inside I wanted to go up to the casket, take the man by the lapel, shake him and ask, "Why? Why? Why did you do this?" Somehow I needed to understand. I needed some way of bringing sanity into an insane moment.

The family tried to give an answer. He'd been to a doctor. The implication was that he had an incurable cancer and chose to save his family the pain of a long drawn-out illness. Maybe that was it, I don't know. In moments that totally confuse us, we need some bit of understanding to cling to so that we can go on, so that we can put some normalcy back into an abnormal world.

Some say that suicide is an unforgivable sin and that it removes that person from the kingdom of God. I don't believe it. I don't believe it because I don't find it in the New Testament. I read in the New Testament that there is only one unforgivable sin and that is to die denying that Christ is Lord, to resist the urging of the Holy Spirit and the grace of God made manifest in Jesus Christ, to deny him throughout one's life even unto death. Even in the face of denial God does not reject the person but the person, by rejecting God's grace, removes himself from the shelter of God's love.

I read in scripture that God forgives. "Lord, how many times shall I forgive my brother when he sins against me, up to seven times? Jesus answered, 'I tell you not seven times but seven times seventy' (Matthew 18:21-22)." I hear the Bible telling us that nothing can separate us from the love of God. "I am convinced that neither death nor life nor angels nor heavenly rulers either present or future nor powers nor height nor depth nor anything else in all creation will be able to separate us from the love of God that is in Christ Jesus our Lord (Romans 8:38-39)."

The man who died wanted to be right with God. Early that morning he went to quiet communion at his church. He went every Wednesday morning for quiet communion. On this day on the bulletin which contained the Order for the Confession of Sins he marked out the word "we" confess and wrote "I" confess. He wanted to be right with God. I pray that he was. I believe that he was. I believe that God in his mercy received him into his kingdom.

Why do I say all of this? Because there are moments like this in all our lives; moments, situations, circumstances that jerk us out of the day-to-day routine and demand that we look at the whole of life. They demand that we recognize the complexity of the human condition and face up to the fact that life is a mystery and we shall never fully understand it. At these moments we are astonished. We are astonished at the gift of life, at the reality of life, and even more astonished at God. We are astonished that in giving life God also gives the freedom to do with it as we will; to use it or abuse it; to invest it or waste it; to live it through to the fullest or to cut it short. We need to understand that life in this world, in this earth and in this body is not forever. It is a brief and temporary moment in time. We are not permanent residents of this place; we are transients who come and go.

A tourist was visiting in the home of a famous rabbi who was known around the world as a wise teacher. The tourist took note of the rabbi's shabby dress and meager surroundings and said to him, "Is this all you have?" The rabbi took note of the tourist's suitcase and replied, "Is this all you have?" The tourist answered, "Why, yes, of course, but I'm only passing through." The rabbi nodded and answered, "So am I!" So are we all only passing through.

The years of youth are wonderful years of life. They are the years of energy, excitement, enthusiasm and creativity. They are the forward-looking years when we don't think much about time, its length or its brevity. In those years time is always ahead of us but at 60 or 70 years time is more precious. We find ourselves looking back as much as forward. We reflect upon what we have done with time rather than what we will do. Do not take time for granted. Do not assume that it will forever stretch out before you. Will Rogers once wrote a poem about time.

The clock of time is wound but once
And no one has the power
To tell just when the hand will stop,
At late or early hour.

Now is the time we have.
Live, love, toil, work with a will.
Do not wait for tomorrow
For the clock may then be still.

Those people who saw the man the day before he went to his office basement, who talked with him, laughed and joked with him, went to lunch with him, saw him at business meetings and civic meetings never once thought that, for him, tomorrow the clock would be still.

Life is God's precious treasure given to each of us. Your time, your physical well being, your love, your friendships, all are parts of God's gift of life to you. Too often we lose those gifts before we begin to value them. In 1911 the Mona Lisa, a magnificant painting, was stolen from the Louvre Museum in Paris. For two years it was gone. The records show that during the two years that it was gone more people came to stare at the blank spot on the wall where the painting had hung than had visited and viewed the Mona Lisa for the previous 12 years. We far too often value and treasure those things that are beautiful, unique and special in our lives after they are gone.

Life is God's treasured gift to you. What shall you do with it? The answer for the Christian is always to give it back. We give it back to the God who gave it. We recommit it and dedicate it to him.

In 1838 Victoria Alexandria was made Queen of England and became known as Queen Victoria. She received many gifts, among them a beautiful diamond. The diamond came as a gift from a small Indian boy. It was of such beauty and value that it became one of the crown jewels. That boy from India grew into a man and became the Maharajah of Punjac. He visited London and asked for an audience with the Queen. During the conversation he asked if he might see the jewel that he had given to her as a child. The diamond was brought out. He held it in his hand for a moment, then knelt before the Queen and said, "Your majesty, when I was but a boy I did not understand the value and worth of this gift that I gave, but now that I am a man I see, recognize and understand its value. Here before you, on my knees, I give it to you again with my love, affection, devotion and loyalty."

Most of us were baptized as children. We did not know or understand the full value of what was being given to God. Now we are older. Now we understand better this treasure of life. Let us go before God once more and say to him, "God, I did not understand the value of the gift of life then, but I understand it better now and understanding its value, I give it to you again with my love, affection, devotion and loyalty."

Many centuries ago Moses, the servant of the Lord, gave back to God the gift of life. Some day, so must we. Let us not have grief in our hearts for, if we belong to him now, we shall belong to him forever. Amen.

Proper 24
Ruth 1:1-19a

Love Without Demand

"But Ruth said . . . where you go I will go, where you stay I will stay; your people will be my people and your God, my God; where you die I will die, and there I will be buried. May the Lord deal with me severely if anything but death separates you and me (Ruth 1:16-17)."

These beautiful words, with the possible exception of 1 Corinthians 13, have been quoted at more weddings than any other text. Even though they have nothing to do with romantic love, they seem right for the occasion because they reflect the highest form of devotion — love without demand.

How many of you can remember your first love? For most, it happened when we were teenagers. We met that very special person who appealed to us in every way and we fell in love. Our new love promised magnificent things — joy, happiness and endless days filled with excitement and anticipation. It was a marvelous experience of waking up to life. For most of us, that first love was short-lived for soon there flooded in upon the relationship hurt and disappointment. The magic seemed to disappear and we discovered that, though love seemed to promise glorious things, it was not able to deliver. Time passed and we became adults. We fell in love again and once more the promise of love was overwhelming. We saw in the other person the opportunity for the fulfillment of our hopes and dreams. The answer to all of life was wrapped in the rainbow of our new love and so we married. After a few years we learned that our hopes were not their hopes and our dreams were not their dreams. We slowly discovered that the experiences of accepting, being close and intimate and being open with another person are the most difficult experiences in life. Once again it appeared that love was able to promise far more than it could produce.

When love fails we withdraw, play it safe and take what is left of our hopes and dreams and, like the man in the parable, bury our talents in the ground. Of course, when we bury what is left of our love we lose it. Many people today feel that they have lost everything and that life is empty. They hear popular songs suggesting that what the world needs now is "love, sweet love." They hear philosophers speak of the beauty of love, psychologists speak of the power of love and the church speaks of the meaning and necessity of love and they wonder, how can I begin to love again?

Jesus said, "Whoever finds his life will lose it, and whoever loses his life for my sake will find it (Matthew 10:39)." In this text, Jesus is offering a starting place for us. He is suggesting that the potential for the growth of love rests in our willingness to give it away. Love is like the air you breathe. If you breathe in and hold your breath, if you never give it back, it will suffocate you.

At this point someone might say, "I give my love away every day. Why then am I not experiencing a deep sense of fulfillment as a person? Why do I still feel empty?" The answer is that most of us give love away in order to receive it. We don't give it freely. We give with strings attached. Many of our expressions of love are designed to reap a reward and to gain a payoff. We touch because we need to be touched. We are kind because we want somebody to be kind to us. We help another because we want them to be in our debt. We give our money as a way of exercising control. Every time we give with the expectation, in fact, with the demand of a return, we transform love into manipulation and we use love to seize control of others.

Some might ask, "Is it possible to give love without expecting a return?" Clearly the love that God gave us in Christ was a love that did not expect return and yet he gave it for our sake. One might reply, "Yes, but that's God and I'm not God. I can't love like God." No, but we can let God love through us and when we do, we are offering love without demand.

There was a young girl, let us call her Jane, who fell in love with a handsome young man. On the evening they were to be married Jane collapsed. At first it appeared that all she needed was a long rest but as time went by her condition degenerated. Jane fell into a deep depression, and she appeared to have lost all contact with the world of reality. She sat in her hospital room staring blankly into space. She would not look at anyone or speak a single word.

Jane remained in that dormant condition for months. One day her psychiatrist told an artist about Jane's condition. The artist asked if he might stop and visit with her. Each day the artist went to her room, sat down in front of her and held out before her eyes a lump of clay. He would work the clay with his fingers. For weeks she gave no indication of seeing the artist or what was in his hand. One day Jane timidly reached out and touched the lump of clay. As time went by she took the clay into her own hands and began to mold it into different shapes and forms. In all those weeks the artist had not spoken to her. He simply trusted in what he could say with his actions.

Finally, one day he softly spoke her name — Jane. Her hands paused, her head came up slowly, and with timid caution she looked at him, the first person she had looked at for months. As he continued to visit with her, the lump of clay became a bond between them. One day she became angry because she could not mold the clay into the shape she wanted. She slammed it to the table and hit it with her fist. The artist smiled and put his hand over hers and said, "You see, Jane,

I like you and believe in you so you don't have to worry when things don't go right." Jane looked up and spoke the first words she had spoken in months, "You like me?" From that point on her progress was rapid and Jane eventually completely recovered.

Observe if you will how the artist expressed his love. He was first patient and silent, never demanding, always willing to let her be where she was for that moment. He did not communicate with her out of his own need. He didn't try to lead her to talk with him so that he would feel important, or respond to him so that he would feel like a great artist. He did not impose on her the need to build his ego. He did not require that she respond to him at all. He simply placed a lump of clay at her disposal. As always, with love, he had to run a risk. He had to take the chance of failure. He had to face the possibility that she might never respond. He was aware from the beginning that he might have to spend weeks and even months in a completely fruitless effort and that all of his love might be poured out to no avail. In his willingness to give his love without demand, he was able to focus all attention on her, on her needs, feelings and potential for recovery.

The result of love without demand was a miracle of rebirth for a girl named Jane. All of us have within us the power to bring about the miracle of rebirth in the lives of others. To the degree we are able to give and to love without demand we will grow in our understanding of what it is to be human and to be a child of God.

I am sure there are many here today who truly desire to give love without demand but every time you try you seem to fail. You get caught in your own selfish needs and in frustration you pull back even further. Don't be surprised at your feelings of frustration when you attempt to give love. Giving doesn't happen automatically. We are not born with the talent. Giving is something that must be learned.

Let me suggest a way for you to start. Begin by looking for ways in which you can give to others without their knowing it. Start with simple things like physical needs — food, clothing or money. Pay for a doctor's bill or provide transportation and do so in a way that the recipient is not aware that you are doing it. Let your giving be a private matter between you and God. Share with God your desire and need to help. Share with him your feelings of failure and your moments of success. Ask God to give you the strength to give more freely of who you are and what you have and thank God for each occasion when you sense that you have truly given without expectation of return.

Once you learn to give material things in an anonymous way you can begin to minister to people's spiritual needs. You can practice encouraging, supporting, listening, caring, accepting and praying for them and believing in them even when they do not believe in themselves. Even spiritual giving can be done anonymously but soon you will learn to do it face-to-face. Every time you give you grow. Every time you give without receiving, you will feel a greater and greater urgency to give again. Slowly your perception of yourself, of life, of love and of God will change. Every time you give you will grow closer to the you that you were meant to be.

To our amazement, a young widow named Ruth, many centuries ago, reflected the grace of God by expressing love without demand. "Where you go I will go; and where you stay I will stay. Your people will be my people and your God my God. Where you die I will die and there will I be buried. May the Lord deal with me severely if anything but death separates you and me (Ruth 1:16-17)." Love without demand; that's how God loves you. Amen.

Under The Wings Of The Almighty

The people of God are strong people. We are not weaklings who tremble and quake every time a new threat comes into our lives. We stand with boldness to face whatever life has to offer. Ruth, the daughter-in-law of Naomi, the woman from the land of Moab, was not a weakling. The death of her husband broke her heart but not her spirit. She was determined to make a new life in a new land. Somehow, the text does not tell us how, Ruth learned to believe in the God of her husband and of her mother-in-law. She learned to trust him as a God of love and compassion. In the words of Boaz, Ruth "sought refuge under the wings of the God of Israel (Ruth 2:12)." Foreigner and convert though she was, Ruth faced the future with courage because she believed her life was under the protection of God.

As Christian people we believe that the Father in heaven answered the prayer of his son, Jesus, when he prayed, "Father, protect them in your name . . . while I was with them I protected them and kept them safe (John 17:11-12)." We face the world with courage today because we are protected by Almighty God.

Robert, a scrawny, 10-year-old boy, answered the knock at the front door. Standing there with hands on hips was the meanest, toughest kid in the neighborhood. "Come on out here," he said, "I'm going to beat you to a bloody pulp." Robert looked up into his face and said, "No, you're not." The bully glared at him angrily and asked, "Why not? You know I'm bigger and meaner than you." "I know," said Robert, "but I also know something that you don't." "What's that?" he sneered. "I know that standing just inside of this door is my big brother." Robert was able to be bold in that moment because his brother, who was bigger than the bully, was nearby. We live our lives with boldness and courage because God is there who is bigger than us and our problems. He is there to protect and defend us.

A woman awakened one morning and heard a pecking sound on the window pane. When she looked she saw a butterfly inside the pane frantically fluttering back and forth. On the other side was a sparrow pecking at the glass trying to catch the butterfly. The butterfly, which couldn't see the pane, thought that he was going to be consumed at any moment by the sparrow. The sparrow thought that at any moment he was going to have a meal; all the while the butterfly was safe because the windowpane was between him and the danger.

God is always between us and the harm and danger of life. We may not always see him. We see the danger; it is there, it's coming, it's approaching, it's in our face, but it never reaches us because God is there to protect and defend us. Someone might say, "Pastor, come on, get real. People are getting hurt and sick and are dying every day. Does God protect them?" My answer is yes; yes, God does protect them. He protects all who love him. Those who live in love live in God and God lives in them. God protects those who trust and believe in him. He protects them not only in life but through life into eternal life. We are always his, "Who shall separate us from the love of Christ? Shall trouble or hardship or persecution or famine or nakedness or danger or sword? As it is written, for your sake we face death all day long. We are considered as sheep to be slaughtered. No, in all these things we are more than conquerors through him who loved us (Romans 8:35-37)." God protects us in life, through life, to eternal life.

God does not change the order of things. Pain and hurt will come to your lives. Death is a part of being human. God doesn't change that but he protects us in it and through it.

We live with boldness because God protects us, not only from the things that are obvious, from the enemies that are always in our faces, but the things that are not obvious — the dangers and threats that we never see. I've often wondered how many thousands of times God has protected my life. He has surely moved me out of harm's way many times when I was not aware.

Workers were preparing to blast rock out of a quarry. They set the dynamite, lit the fuse and ran for cover. When they looked back they saw a little three-year-old boy wandering out into the open field. They knew that any second the dynamite would explode; the little boy's life was in danger. They stood and frantically waved, trying to get the little boy to come to them. The boy was amused by their antics and went right on playing. His life was in danger but none of the men had the courage to rush out and rescue him; they knew the dynamite was getting ready to explode. The little boy's mother came on the scene and at a glance realized what was happening. She did not call out to her son nor rush out to get him. In her mother's love and intuition she simply knelt down, opened her arms wide and smiled at him, beckoning him to come. Instantly the little boy ran toward his mother. The dynamite exploded, sending a shockwave reverberating off the walls of the canyon, but the little boy was safe in his mother's arms. He never knew he was in danger; the only thing he saw was the beckoning arms of his loving mother. How many times do we hear God call to us, beckoning us to himself and all we hear is his love. We are not aware that he is at the same time beckoning us away from some harm or hurt that may lie in our path.

Many people have said, "You know, Pastor, I haven't been to church in many years but I felt an urgency to come to church today, and I want you to know what a great moment it has been. I feel renewed in my faith in God and know my life will be altogether different." I often wonder if these people realize that not only are they experiencing the beckoning call of God to come to him, but that he's also calling them away from a path in life that would harm and hurt.

The late Peter Marshall, the famous Presbyterian pastor, once described an occasion when he was a boy. He was walking home in Scotland in the darkness when he suddenly stumbled and fell. As he reached out his hand in front to brace himself and stand up, there was nothing there! Frightened, he simply remained in that position until the morning. In the early light of day he could see that he had fallen at the edge of a high cliff. One more step and he would have fallen to his death. He determined then and there that if God could guide his steps in the darkness of night, he would certainly follow God in the light of day.

There are times when it becomes abundantly clear to us that God is leading our steps and protecting our path. At one of the shopping centers in the city of Atlanta, a man named James Calvin Brady went berserk and shot five people; one of them died. In a newspaper interview, Brady acknowledged that at an earlier time he had gone to the mall with a gun in hand determined to fire 12 bullets, implying he determined to kill 12 people. He said that on that day he walked into the mall and stood before the escalator, planning to shoot the people as they came down. Something happened, however, something changed his mind and he put the gun away and left. My guess is that the people on the escalator that day never knew their lives were in danger. They rode down the escalator laughing and talking among themselves. They thought ahead to the gifts they would buy or the shops they would enter. They went home, fixed dinner, spent time with their families, went to bed and had a peaceful night's rest. They never knew, and still don't, that they were within seconds of death. How many times have we been protected by God and did not even know it?

Many years ago two brothers played golf every day for seven days on a beautiful course on the island of St. Croix. Every day they had lunch on the veranda at the club house. The week after they returned home, the paper reported that a gang of thieves had come out of the jungle around the golf course and attacked people on the veranda, killing everyone who was there. The thieves killed the woman who had waited on the two brothers, the young golf pro who had helped them, and the men and women who had served them lunch. The brothers could not help but wonder how close they came to death. They could have gone on their trip a week later and been sitting on the veranda that fateful day. They wondered if it was possible that the gang had planned their attack the week before and at the last moment something happened that changed their minds. How many, many times in life has God protected us all and we did not even know it?

What is our proper response to a God who loves us so much and protects us at all times? The one appropriate response is thanksgiving. Deep in our hearts we need to learn to be thankful to God.

Martin Luther loved to tell the story about the two bishops who were riding down the road on horeseback and saw a shepherd in the field. The shepherd was crying, weeping and wailing with tears pouring down his face. One of the bishops, a man of kind heart, rode over to ask the shepherd about his problem. The shepherd was sobbing so loudly that he could barely speak, but he pointed to the ground. The bishop saw a small toad sitting in the grass. The shepherd said, "All this time Almighty God has treated me with such good favor. He has blessed me in so many ways, not like that poor miserable toad on the ground, and yet I have never expressed to him my thanksgiving or praised his holy name."

Martin Luther, in commenting about this scene, pointed out that this was not a man of power; he was not a man of wealth; he was not even a man of learning. He was a humble shepherd and yet so understood the grace and love of God that he wept tears of thanksgiving.

I've wondered, where are our tears? Where are our tears of thanksgiving? We who take God's protective love so for granted, we who have been blessed by God in so many ways, where are our tears of thanksgiving?

A famous speaker once asked his audience, "Do you give thanks to God every morning for your health and for your life? No," he said, "I didn't either for a long time but then I had by-pass surgery. Now I do, every single day."

In this harsh world I try to say to parents, "Parents, love your children, be good to them, thank God that they are well and healthy and that you still have them with you and have not lost them." Across the years I've been with far too many parents who have. I say to children, "Love your parents, honor your parents, thank God for your parents and do it now." Over the years, I have known far too many who waited until it was too late.

There are times when tears are good. One of those times is when we shed them giving thanks to God for his blessings. As people of God we live boldly with courage and confidence. We are not weaklings! We will not tremble and quake when some new threat enters our lives.

Like Ruth of long ago, many things will break our hearts but nothing can break our spirits, for we have found refuge under the wings of Almighty God. Amen.

34

Chosen By God

All of us love to be chosen. It is a wonderful thing to be chosen. A teen-age boy tried out for the basketball team. When the coach posted the list of those who had made the team, he was thrilled to discover that the coach had chosen him. A young woman was one of 75 applicants for a high-paying job. She exclaimed with great excitement in her voice, "Of all the applicants, they chose me." A young friend who had made application to the Naval Academy announced with great pride that out of the hundreds who had applied, "They chose me." It's a great thing to be chosen. It makes us feel good; it makes us feel wanted, needed and valued. It makes us feel special.

We learn in the beginning of the book of Ruth that she did not feel very special. Her young husband died leaving her alone and destitute. When her world suddenly turned upside down, Ruth determined to leave homeland behind and cast her future with her mother-in-law, Naomi. She was forced, for the sake of survival, to impose upon the charity of her kinsman, Boaz, who permitted her to gather leftover grain in the field. When compared to the giants of the covenant like Abraham, Isaac, Jacob and Moses, the Moabite woman, Ruth, seems insignificant and out of place as a main character in the Bible. She was a foreigner whose only claim to remembrance

35

was her devotion to her mother-in-law and her cleverness in securing a husband.

Ruth didn't feel very special but she was. In Matthew's gospel we learn why. Ruth, the pitiful widow from Moab, through her marriage to Boaz and the birth of her son, Obed, was eventually to be the great-grandmother of King David. King David was of the royal lineage of our Lord Jesus Christ. Ruth was chosen by God to be an instrument of his grace in sending his son, Jesus, into our world.

Why did God choose Ruth? Was she a powerful leader of the people? Was she a profoundly spiritual person? Did she come from a noble family? No, she was none of these things. She was a quiet, ordinary woman who lost her husband and struggled to survive in a foreign land.

The answer is we don't know why God chose Ruth. We only know that he did. We might also ask, why did God choose you? As a child of God you are the beneficiary of his grace, love, salvation and eternal life. Why did God choose you? Because you are good; because you are righteous; because you are profoundly spiritual? The truth is we don't really know why God chose you; we only know that he did.

What does it mean to be chosen by God? To be chosen by God is an intensely personal thing. The New Testament declares that Jesus died for the world, that he died for the church, that he died for the kingdom, but do not ever forget that the bottom line of faith is this, Jesus died for you. Faith is an intensely personal matter between you and your God. No one else can believe for you; no one else can trust or love for you; no one else can laugh or cry for you; no one else can live or die for you; no one else can stand before God in your place. You are a person — one lone, solitary individual — who is sometimes brave, sometimes scared, sometimes glad and sometimes sad. You are a person and your life with all of its marvelous complexity belongs to you, and your life is important to God.

Yes, God reaches out to the world, to nations, to races, to groups large and small, but remember he reaches out to you.

God knows your name. He understands the feelings in your heart and the substance in your soul. Your laughter fills his divine being and your tears break his sacred heart. You are a person — a complex, often confused, frequently hurt, sometimes glad, occasionally successful — person. Don't be afraid to be human. Don't be afraid to be you, the person that you are.

The world, including the world of the church, will often misunderstand, criticize, judge and even condemn you. Accept those feelings. They are the price you pay for being human. Do not hold a grudge against those who misunderstand. They, too, have their burdens to bear. Remember, God blessed the human condition by sending his son to be human.

Now is a good time to shed the pretense of life. There is no need for you to strive to be a super Christian or super-righteous person. It is enough to be human, to be authentically human. We are what we are, dear friends, nothing more, nothing less, strangers traveling through a strange land in search of our home with God. To be chosen by God is an intensely personal thing.

To be chosen by God can also be an extremely painful thing. Jesus said, "If anyone would believe in me, let him take up his cross and follow me (Matthew 16:24)." The cross is a symbol of suffering and an instrument of pain. If you love others, you share their hurts, their sorrows and their pain. To be chosen by God can be a painful thing. Know that it can. Be aware of it. Expect it.

Can you imagine what it is like for a pastor to have to go to a family and announce to them "Your teenage son has been killed in a car accident." To be chosen can be a painful thing. What must it be like for a doctor to say to his patient, "I'm sorry, but the results of the biopsy indicate that you have a malignant growth and there is nothing we can do about it." Can you imagine what it was like for the soldiers who fought in the Persian Gulf? Many were Christian people who loved God, trusted in Christ and yet they were required to take up arms against their fellow human beings and even take the lives of others. To be chosen to serve can be a painful thing.

I read about two policemen who were called to a disturbance on the street. A young man was waving a gun in the air. People were hiding behind cars or wherever they could. The policemen took cover and shouted to the young man, "Put down the gun, put it down." The young man continued to wave the gun in the air. They tried again, "Put down the gun." The young man ignored their command and pointed the gun straight at one of the policemen. In a reflex action the policeman shot and killed him. They later discovered that the gun was a toy and that the young man was retarded and did not understand. To serve others is a painful thing!

A woman told me about being with her mother through the final weeks of a terminal illness. The family tried to sit with her 24 hours a day. The mother had difficulty going to sleep and was awake almost constantly. The woman said, "We came down to the last few days. I had been with my mother all that day, and about 3 a.m. I drifted off to sleep. My mother awakened me and asked, 'Can you not stay awake with me these last hours?' " How reminiscent of Peter, James and John in the Garden of Gethsemane when Christ came to them and said, "Can you not watch with me just one hour?" To be chosen can be a painful thing! To be chosen by God is a very personal thing and it can be a painful thing.

To be chosen by God is a most demanding thing. Remember, God, in choosing you, gives you everything. He gives you his grace and love, salvation and eternal life and the gift of the Holy Spirit. He gives you everything and expects everything in return. When you accept the blessing of God, you also accept the responsibility that is attendant to that blessing.

Your congregation was chosen to be the church where you are in this time in history and therefore carries a great responsibility. You must be the best, strongest, most loving, giving, caring church that you can be. Why? Because so much depends on it. Thousands upon thousands of lives are touched by your church and its ministry across the period of a year.

Think of the challenges that are always before our society. We dare not face those challenges as a weak and feeble church. Young people need the church now more than ever. Statistics tell us that in the next 24 hours in this country, 3,200 children and teenagers will run away from home, 2,900 will see their parents divorced, 2,800 teenage girls will become pregnant, 1,850 children will be abused or neglected, 1,500 teenagers will drop out of school, 1,100 teenage girls will have an abortion, 200 children will be arrested for drug abuse, and six teenagers will commit suicide. Can we face that challenge as a weakened, enfeebled church? Understand that to be chosen of God is a demanding thing.

To be chosen by God is a wonderfully glorious thing. You are chosen by God; you are not chosen by a wealthy employer, an important person, or even a dear friend . . . you are chosen by God. You are chosen for his love and grace, for his gifts and blessings. To be chosen by God is an incredibly glorious thing.

A young boy kept making mistakes while practicing the piano to perform at a recital. His mother advised, "Son, practice the end of your recital piece. Practice the closing measures as hard as you can, over and over again, because the truth is, you can make mistakes in the beginning, you can make mistakes in the middle, but people will forget all of that if you make the end glorious!"

I don't know what the beginning was like for you. I don't know what your childhood was like or what mistakes were made. I don't know where you are or what mistakes you've recently made but I can tell you, wherever you are, Christ is with you. If you will trust him and love him, he will make the end glorious.

Long ago God chose a quiet, ordinary woman named Ruth who had lost her husband and was struggling to survive in a foreign land to be an instrument of his grace in bringing his son, Jesus, into the world. We don't know why God chose Ruth. We only know that he did. Today he chooses you, an ordinary person struggling to survive in a difficult world, as an instrument of his grace in bringing his son, Christ, to the world. We don't know why God has chosen you; we only know that he has. Amen.

Life Isn't Fair

The story is told of the old Irishman who was critically ill. The family called the priest. The priest, in preparation for the last rites, asked the obvious and expected question, "O'Riley," he said, "do you desire to renounce the devil and all his works?" O'Riley, who was fully conscious, thought for a moment and said, "Frankly, Father, considering the condition I'm in, I'd rather not antagonize anyone right now."

The children of Israel were having a tough time and given the conditions they were in, they could ill afford to antagonize anyone, especially God, but they did. Amos, the prophet, pleaded with them to return to God with their whole heart. He reminded them that they had abandoned God and forsaken his covenant. They performed religious rituals at the holy shrines and bragged about how righteous they were. They lived in luxury, took bribes and cheated the poor. In ignorant arrogance they "longed for the day of the Lord (Amos 5:18)." Amos warned them "that day will be darkness not light. It will be as though a man fled from a lion only to meet a bear . . . Though you bring burnt offerings and grain offerings, I will not accept them. Let justice roll on like a river and righteousness like a never failing stream (Amos 5:18-24)." The people thought that because they were God's people they were

41

favored and privileged and no harm would come to them. When famine, drought, locusts and the ravages of war came they grumbled and protested. They complained that life isn't fair, that God speaks of justice but there's no justice for them. We are his people, they thought, and yet he rains sorrow on our heads.

Life isn't fair. They are, of course, right — life isn't fair. It never is. Do not expect it to be. Do not plan on it, do not count on it, because life is not fair. Life does not care who you are, does not care whether you are good or bad, right or wrong, faithful or unfaithful. Life is not fair! Life will knock you down, step on you, kick you in the side, and then run over you for good measure — there's nothing fair about life.

Was life fair to the young mother who drove up to the stoplight to wait for the traffic to move and a man walked up, jerked open the door of her car, snatched her purse and shot her to death? Was life fair for her?

Was life fair to the school teacher who was waiting at the train station for his wife to come from her job and a gang of teenagers beat him and shot him to death? The tragedy was only increased by the realization that the man was a teacher who gave his time and energy for teenagers in his church and his school. Was life fair for him or his family?

Was life fair for the world-class Olympic athlete who suffered an injury while playing on a trampoline that left him a quadriplegic? Was life fair for him?

Was life fair to the brilliant young surgeon who had the God-given talent to save people's lives who suffered a rare illness and was left totally blind? Was life fair for him?

Was life fair to the man who worked 45 years on the same job and finally retired so he could have some time to do all the things he wanted to do only to suffer a stroke one week later that left him paralyzed? Was life fair to him?

Was life fair to the lovely young girl who was in an automobile accident and suffered a head injury and has been in a coma for months? Was life fair to her?

No, life is not fair. Do not count on it, do not expect it — life is not fair. Life is a reflection of us, of what we are — of our sinful nature and our broken world. There is nothing in this broken world that is fair. God is fair. Life is not fair, but God is fair. God is more than fair — God goes beyond what is fair. God heals, helps, loves, guides, directs, strengthens, comforts, forgives and when everything else fails and we still stray from him and disobey him, God has mercy.

The people of Israel turned away from God, broke every commandment and made a mockery of worship. The fair thing would have been for God to turn away from them forever and to abandon them in their misery but God is more than fair, he is merciful. Over and over again he said to the people, "Seek me and live (Amos 5:4)." "The days are coming," declares the Lord, "when I will bring back my exiled people, Israel. They will rebuild their own cities and live in them, they will plant vineyards and drink their wine. They will make gardens and eat their food (Amos 9:13-14)."

God is fair, he is more than fair. He goes from what is fair to what is good, to what is gracious, to what is loving. Remember when you are struggling in the darkness of life, when you cry out in the night hours of your grief, when you face the hardships of the day, remember, life is not fair but God is.

How do we know that God is fair? He sent his son, Jesus Christ, to tell us, to be with us, to share the journey and to sustain and strengthen us. The signs of God's presence have always been with his people. Did he not make a covenant with Abraham? Did he not send his angel to wrestle with Jacob at the Brook Jabbok? Did he not send Moses to lead them out of bondage in Egypt? Did he not give them manna when they were hungry and springs of water when they were thirsty? Did he not give them the ten commandments as an expression of his covenant? Did he not send his prophet Amos to call the people to repentance? The signs of his presence were everywhere.

The same signs are here today. They are here when we pray for each other, when we support and encourage each other, when we reach out a hand to the lonely or offer food to the hungry. The signs of God's presence are with us telling us we do not journey alone. God is fair, more than fair. God goes beyond what is fair to what is good.

Though it was difficult for the people of Israel, they had to learn that God is good to everyone. His love is not limited to an exclusive few. There is not a certain group of people who are our kind of people. All people are our kind of people. Jesus said so in the gospel of John. "For God so loved the world that he gave his only son that if anyone believes in him, they will not perish but have eternal life (John 3:16)." The New English translates the text, ". . . that everyone who has faith in him may not die." The Revised Standard version translates, the text ". . . whoever believes in him shall not perish." The King James version reads, ". . . whosoever believeth in him . . ." Normally I prefer a more contemporary version but for this text I love the King James and that wonderful, beautiful, powerful word "whosoever." It has substance to it — there are no limits to it. It reaches to the height and depth and breadth of the whole world. It includes everyone, no one is excluded!

"Whosoever believes." The text does not say whosoever likes the old hymnal, or whosoever likes the new hymnal, or whosoever believes in infant baptism, or whosoever believes in adult baptism or whosoever serves grape juice with communion or whosoever serves wine with communion or whosoever has red doors on their church or whosoever has clergy who wear robes. The passage says simply "whosoever believes."

Who are the whosoevers? Are they the Afro-Americans? Are they Scandinavian, Oriental, European, Hispanic? Yes, by all means. Are they rich? Yes. Are they poor, middle class? By all means. Are they young; are they old; are they the baby boomers? Certainly. Are they the happy, the sad, the miserable, the glad, the hurting, the suffering sinners? Yes, of course.

Are they the single, the married, the divorced, the widowed? Yes. The Word is clear in its breadth and in its power, "whosoever believes in him."

How is that possible? It is possible because there are no barriers. There are no barriers at the cross. There is no wall, there is no fence to keep certain ones away. "Whosoever" may go there, kneel, repent and discover the freedom that is in that cross. "Whosoever" may go to the empty tomb; there is no barrier there; the stone has been rolled away. "Whosoever" may enter and see that Christ has risen. The wonderful word "whosoever" includes you and me. We can go to the cross, kneel, confess and discover again the love and grace of God.

We are shocked every day with some new and painful reminder that life isn't fair. Our hope is not in life but in God for we know and believe that God is fair — he is more than fair, he is good. His goodness is for all and it endures forever. Amen.

Proper 28
Zephaniah 1:7, 12-18

When God Has Enough

There was no doubt in Zephaniah's mind that God had had enough. His people bowed down to other gods and no longer turned to the Lord in prayer nor did they seek his help. They blindly walked their own selfish and greedy path and in their arrogance thought God would sit quietly by and do nothing. They were wrong! "Listen, the cry on the day of the Lord will be bitter . . .that day will be a day of wrath, a day of distress and anguish . . . (Zephaniah 1:14-15)." Our Lord Jesus in similar fashion spoke to the world of his day, "I did not come to bring peace but a sword (Matthew 10:34)."

Christians are frequently shocked when they come across biblical passages which suggest that God has had enough. We prefer to remember that we are blessed of God and forgiven of our sins. We remind ourselves that we have been given the fruits of the Spirit — love, joy, peace, patience, kindness, goodness, faithfulness, gentleness and self-control (Galatians 5:22-23) and that Jesus said, "Peace I give to you (John 14:2)."

We have trouble accepting the paradox that we live in faith and yet in sin, that we are children of the kingdom of God and yet citizens of this world. The New Testament tells us that the ruler of this present darkness is Satan. Whether we use the name Beelzebub, Lucifer, the Devil, Force of Evil or some other designation, the truth remains that the world in which we live is under an evil power. It is broken, shattered and corrupt.

The truth is we do not have to be convinced of the brokenness of our world, do we? We experience it in our own lives every day. We are like the Indian who was laying on the ground with his ear close to the earth. A cowboy came along and saw him. When he heard the Indian muttering, he moved closer to see if he could hear what he was saying. The Indian grumbled, "Stagecoach headed west; four horses — three gray, one white; two drivers; four passengers, three men, one woman." The cowboy in astonishment asked, "My goodness, you mean you can tell all of that from listening to the ground?" "No," said the Indian, "Stagecoach ran over me 30 minutes ago." We know what it's like for the four horses and the stagecoach of life to run over us and leave us face down in the dust.

If a few moments pass when we are not overwhelmed by the brokenness of life in our personal experiences, we read about it in the experiences of others. A few years ago we all saw the incredibly shocking videotape that was distributed by the media throughout the world. It was a tape made by a group of terrorists who held an American officer as a hostage. In order to make their point, they hanged him, videotaped his death and sent it to the world to see. Surely it is a broken and violent world in which we live.

In the city of Atlanta a young woman, obviously out of her mind, killed her two children and threw herself in front of the rapid transit train to commit suicide. I read not long ago about a father who deliberately drove the family car into the lake in an attempt to kill them all. Miraculously, all but an eight-year-old boy survived. The broken nature of our world is profoundly clear.

Zephaniah is telling us in the text for today that God will not make peace with a broken world. He will not make peace with evil. Jesus supported the words of Zephaniah by saying, "I came not to bring peace but a sword (Matthew 10:34)." The sword of which he speaks is the sword of the Spirit. What

48

is the sword of the Spirit? It is the Word of God which conveys his grace, power and righteous will.

We must understand that Jesus did not come to this broken world to destroy it, but to redeem, conquer, transform and change the world for the glory of his father in heaven. We do not always believe that we need to be changed. We oftentimes resist change even though it is for our own good.

If you were to take a trip to Enterprise, Alabama, and ride through the town square, you would see a most unusual monument. The people of Enterprise have erected a monument to the boll weevil. The story behind the monument suggests that in 1915 the boll weevil totally destroyed the cotton crop in Coffey County, Alabama. Cotton was the only crop grown in the entire county and everyone in it was economically devastated. The people decided this would never happen again and began to diversify and plant other crops. Soon they discovered that by diversifying they had a stronger, healthier, more stable economy and were far better off. As a result, they dedicated a monument to the boll weevil and thanked God for the little creature of destruction for if it had not come, they would have never changed.

We are in some respects like those people. We struggle along our narrow path not realizing the need for change. Thank God Jesus Christ has come to change us and show us a new and better way of life. That new and better life begins when we hear the words of Zephaniah and repent, and when we hear our Lord Jesus Christ calling us to take up the cross and follow him.

The truth is we need someone to follow in our world today. There is no real leader to whom we can turn. I saw a bumper sticker recently that read, "Don't follow me, I'm lost too." Everyone appears to be following everyone else and no one seems to know where anyone is going. There is a significant absence of leadership. We turn to the politicians and feel deceived. We turn to the religious leaders and feel betrayed. We turn to the scientists and find that they can lead us no further than the limits of the physical world. We turn to the economists and find that the poor are getting poorer. There is a vacuum of leadership in the world today and the church is doing little more than standing by as a passive observer.

The time has come for the church to step into the vacuum, not to lift up self but to lift up Christ the Savior of the world. The only one who can lead us is the Lord Jesus Christ. Did he not say, "I am the way, the truth and the life (John 14:6)?" Jesus Christ knows where he is going and knows how to lead the way. Take up your cross and follow him.

Phillips Brooks was one of the best-known pastors of the last century. We perhaps know him best as the man who wrote the Christmas carol, "O Little Town of Bethlehem." The story is told that when Phillips Brooks came to the end of life, he was gravely ill and could not receive visitors. Many of his dearest friends came to his home but were not given admittance because he was simply too ill to see them. Among those who came, however, was a man named Robert Ingersoll. Ingersoll was the best-known atheist of his day and yet he and Phillips Brooks were close friends. When he came, to his surprise, he was immediately shown into the sick room. "Phillips, I know so many of your other friends were not given audience. Why are you willing to see me?" Phillips Brooks replied, "My dear friend Robert, I will see most of my other friends in the life to come but it occurred to me this might be my last opportunity to speak to you." Phillips Brooks knew where he was going. Long ago he had taken up the cross to follow Christ.

As we take up our cross to embark on our journey, we need to understand that it begins in worship where we dedicate our lives anew in his presence.

In 1620 the Pilgrims gathered to climb aboard the Mayflower and set sail for a new world. They gathered for a final service of worship with their pastor, John Robinson. On that momentous occasion he spoke to them with heartfelt emotion. "My friends, this is a most important service of worship for before we gather again we will have embarked on a dangerous and strange journey." He paused for a moment and then concluded, "Every time we gather for worship is important because, and who knows, between the time we gather here and the time we will gather again, who among us will have embarked on some new and glorious journey."

Every time we gather for worship we gather in the knowledge that perhaps before we gather again someone known to us, some dear friend or loved one, will have embarked on a new and glorious journey. Every time we come for worship, let us renew our commitment for the journey with Christ and take up our cross and follow him.

Two thousand years ago Jesus issued a warning to the broken and sinful world. "I did not come to bring peace but a sword (Matthew 10:34)." Hundreds of years before Christ, Zephaniah warned the people that "the day of the Lord would be bitter (Zephaniah 1:14)."

As we struggle with the brokenness of this world, let us remember that war and bitterness are never the last words in the life of one who loves God and trusts in Christ Jesus. Zephaniah concluded his work with the thought, "On that day they will say to Jerusalem, do not fear, oh Zion, do not let your hands hang limp. The Lord your God is with you. He is mighty to save you. He will take great delight in you. He will quiet you with his love. He will rejoice over you with singing (Zephaniah 3:16-17)."

Our Lord Jesus Christ said to his followers, "Come to me all ye who are weary and burdened and I will give you rest. Take my yoke upon you and learn from me for I am gentle and humble in heart and you will find rest for your souls (Matthew 11:28-29)." There is no doubt that Zephaniah, those many years ago, was right. God had had enough. He had had enough of watching the brokenness and pain of his people. In due time, according to his will, he sent his son to set us free. Believe in him and the peace that passes all understanding. Amen.

The Call To Victory

The book of Revelation is a powerful and beautiful book designed to answer one question. The people of the early church were suffering under persecution and many were being martyred. They looked for the second coming of Christ as the grand and glorious answer to their pain. They asked the question, "How long will it be before Christ returns? How long will it be before the victory is final and complete?" The book of Revelation gives a clear and simple answer: "Behold, I am coming soon (Revelation 22:12)."

For the Christian, all of life is lived based upon this simple promise. In Revelation 7:9-17 the promise has been heard, believed and celebrated. "Salvation belongs to our God who sits on the throne and to the Lamb (Revelation 7:10)." The saints of God celebrate his eternal victory before there is a new heaven and a new earth, before there is a new Jerusalem coming down out of the sky, before there is a river of life flowing from the throne of God. The people of God celebrate as if it has already happened, for indeed, for the faithful it has.

A pastor had been invited to give the invocation at an athletic field used for the Special Olympics. Eight hundred special athletes came to participate in games designed just for them. The events started with a parade of athletes; 800 young men and women made their way around the track, banners held high and flags waving, cheering as they went. Some of them limped, some had braces on their legs and used crutches to walk. Others had arms that dangled uselessly by their sides. Some were in wheelchairs and had to be pushed but they were all there filled with the excitement of the games that were to come. Finally, they made their way around the track and into the main grandstand to await the beginning of the games.

Everyone looked down to the right corner for the entry of the olympic torch. A young teenage boy named Joel entered the stadium and began to run around the track with the torch held high. The farther Joel went the faster he ran until finally he was running as hard as he could go. The people in the stands began to catch the excitement of this young man and his run to the finish line and the platform. They stood and began to applaud, then to yell and finally to cheer. Young Joel came down before the stands, ran up the platform and at the top, turned and in true Rocky fashion, jumping up and down waving his arms, he thrust the torch in the air as high as it would go.

As the spectacle unfolded, one word came to mind — victory. Victory — they had already won it! Before the games start, before the first race is run, before any one of them grows too weak and tired to finish that race, before anyone finished last, victory had already been won. Victory was in the air, it was in their faces, it was in their voices, in truth it was in their hearts.

Eight hundred special athletes, bedraggled, maimed, crippled, and yet they stood and cheered young Joel. Why? Because, regardless of the outcome of the games, they had already won. That, my friends, is the spirit of the book of Revelation. It is the spirit of the Christian life. For all of us who have been baptized, before the games of life ever begin, we have already won the victory.

Victory is what All Saints Sunday is all about. Victory is in the air this morning, it is in our faces, it is in our voices, and in truth it is in our hearts. We have already won. Our loved ones who died during this past year have lost nothing but have in fact gone on to claim the crown of righteousness which the righteous judge has kept for them.

We, too, have already won, before we lose that job, before the heart attack, before the operation, before the sorrow of grief, before failure with our children or spouse or self, before those feelings of being lost and lonely, before we wonder if we will ever smile again. Before any of that, the faith in our hearts cries out, "Victory!"

The victory was won on that first Easter Day. The stone was rolled away, the tomb is empty, he is not here, he is risen. On that first resurrection day God, through his Son, Jesus Christ, proclaimed victory forever and nothing can change it. Nothing can ever set it aside.

Why is it so important for us to know, believe and trust the promise of Revelation and the trust of Easter? It is important for you to know and trust so that when you run the race of life, when you stumble and fall, when you are hurt or injured, when things don't work out and you finish last, you still know that you are not defeated. You are not defeated for, regardless of the outcome or the course of human events, the one victory that really counts, that is above every victory, has already been won. Listen, listen, my friends, the world stands before us and shouts hate but God whispers love. The world shouts doubt but God whispers faith. The world shouts defeat but God whispers victory, victory!

Do not ever surrender your life to the power of darkness, despair or defeat. You are resurrection people. You have been given a different view. You no longer have to look out of the window of darkness and despair. You have been shown a new window where there is light, hope and victory.

A little girl was standing at a window; it was dark and cloudy outside, tears were streaming down her face. She wept as she watched her father and her big brother bury in the back-yard her closest friend, her little puppy. Her grandfather came and stood beside her for a few moments. Understanding her grief he reached down and gently took her hand and led her through the house to another room, to another window, a window that looked out across the front yard and her mother's flower garden. He knelt down beside her and pointed to a little spring flower that was just beginning to push its head above the soil and whispered to her, "My dear, you have been looking out of the wrong window."

God comes to us when we look out of the window of darkness and despair and takes us by the hand and gently leads us to another place, shows us another window and whispers to us, "My dear children, you have been looking out of the wrong window. Let me show you a new window where there is light, life and victory for all."

John Quincy Adams was one of the early presidents of our country. When he was very old, he endured a particularly bad winter. He was in bed for months. When spring came he was determined to go for a walk and, with the aid of his cane, he made his way slowly down the street. A friend passing by said to him, "Well, tell me, how is John Adams today?" The old gentleman replied, "If you're asking about this old house in which John Adams lives, I can tell you it is in pretty bad shape — the windows are broken out, the roof is caving in, I can't remember anything any more. The foundations are weak and tottery. Why 'most any wind that comes along makes this old house shake and tremble. I dare say that this house is in such ill condition that no doubt its tenant will soon be moving out. But, if you're asking about John Adams himself, then I can tell you he's all right and will be a thousand years from now."

Do you hear it? Do you hear the note that he sounds? The note of victory? It's the same note that we hear from the apostle Paul when he says, "I have fought the good fight, I have finished the race, I have kept the faith; now I go to receive the victory, the crown of righteousness which the Lord, the Righteous Judge, will award me on that day and not only to me but also to all who have longed for his appearing (2 Timothy 4:6-8)." Do you hear it? Do you hear the note of victory that is sounded, the same note that was heard that day from 800 special children as they gathered for their own olympic festival?

Have you not noticed that Easter always comes early? Our celebration of the resurrection always comes before Good Friday, Holy Week, Lent, before Ash Wednesday. The resurrection of Christ is celebrated any time anywhere Christian people proclaim the great victory of God.

Dear friends, we live in a world that has become accustomed to defeat. The people around us have made peace with darkness and gloom as if despair is their only choice. It isn't, we know it isn't. The victory of God is for all his children. Go with your light into the darkness, share it, proclaim it, give it, and live it victoriously. Amen.

The Shepherd King

There is a wonderful story out of the 16th century about Bishop Hugh Latimer, a great leader of the church. One Sunday morning he entered his pulpit and looked out to see King Henry VIII in the congregation. He knew that what he had to say that day would not go well with King Henry. He thought for a moment and then said to himself, but out loud for all to hear, "Latimer, be careful what you say today; King Henry is here." He thought for a moment longer and again said to himself, but aloud so others could hear, "Latimer, be careful what you say today; the King of kings is here."

Today the King of kings is here and we have come together to celebrate his presence, power, majesty and glory in our world and in our lives. For us Jesus Christ is truly the "King of kings, the Lord of lords, and he shall reign forever and ever. Alleluia!"

Christ our King is here with us today. Can't you feel his presence when you enter this place of worship, when you kneel or pray, or lift your voice in song? Can't you feel the presence of the King? He is here. He is sitting there beside you. Can't you feel it? He is standing here beside me. When we kneel, he kneels with us. I know he is here because he promised, "Lo, I am with you always (Matthew 28:20)." "When two or three are gathered in my name, there I will be also (Matthew 18:20)."

The King of kings is here with us today! He is not way out there somewhere in space ruling from a distant throne. He is not a God who is remote and removed from his people. He is the imminent God, the God with us here and now. He is a God who loves and protects us. He is the great "Shepherd King."

We have a beautiful presentation of the Shepherd King in Ezekiel, chapter 34. God says, "I will be the shepherd of my sheep . . . I will seek the lost. I will bring back those who have strayed. I will bind up the crippled. I will strengthen the weak (Ezekiel 34:15-16)."

Our King is like a shepherd who has come to love us and to lead us. Think with me for a few moments about what it means for the king, the shepherd, to lead his people. We are called to follow him wherever he goes, wherever the path may lead.

We learn in life that the path of faith is not always an easy one to walk. Years ago a missionary society in South Africa wrote a letter to David Livingstone in which they inquired, "Have you found a good road that leads to where you are? We have some men who wish to join you." Livingstone wrote back, "If the men you want to send will come only if there is a good road, do not send them. I don't want them. I need men who will come even if there is no road at all."

Friends, we are called to follow our Lord Jesus Christ, the great king and shepherd, even if there is no road at all. He came into our world "to lead us by the still waters, to restore our souls, to lead us in the paths of righteousness for his name's sake (Psalm 23)."

We find that it is just as difficult to follow the lead of our King today as it was 2,000 years ago for the first disciples. We, too, are asked to give all that we are — heart, mind, body, soul and strength — to him. We are called to follow him regardless of the cost of our discipleship.

In his sermon one Sunday, a pastor was telling his congregation that they needed to give 10 percent of their income to Christ and to the work of his church. Among those in the congregation was a man who fit the description of a yuppie. He was young, bright and successful. He had an excellent job which provided a substantial income. He owned a beautiful new Mercedes. He was touched by the sermon and wanted to take the pastor seriously. Following the service, he went to the pastor and said, "I really want to tithe, I want to give 10 percent of what I have to the church, but if I do I will not be able to make the payment each month on my Mercedes." The pastor replied, "It seems to me that you have only one choice and that is to sell the Mercedes." The young man shook his head and walked slowly away. Two weeks later the pastor saw the young man again and inquired, "John, I was wondering, did you ever make a decision about tithing?" The young man smiled and replied, "Yes, Pastor, I did. I sold the Mercedes." We might think that to give up the Mercedes wasn't much of a sacrifice, but try it! Try it! Try selling something that you treasure and value in order that you may tithe. Try it and then tell me how easy it is to follow wherever the Shepherd leads.

There are times, dear friends, when we are called to sacrifice, to pay some heavy cost in order to follow the King, but we follow because we know the King has walked the hard road before us. He has gone ahead of us. He has already made the sacrifice. He has already experienced the hardships of the journey. He has already suffered the pain of the road for our sake.

Centuries ago, Saint Martin of Tours sat in his prison cell. There was a knock at the door. A mysterious figure stood before him. Saint Martin could not recognize the mysterious figure so he asked, "Tell me, who are you?" The answer came back, "I am your Savior." Saint Martin was not convinced and asked a second question: "Then where are the prints of the nails?" The mysterious visitor vanished. There can be no savior without the prints of the nails. There is no discipleship without cost.

We are called to follow where our Shepherd King leads. We follow where he leads but we follow with joy in our hearts. Though the way may be hard and painful for us, we follow with joy in our hearts because we travel with the King. The King is with us; we cannot be defeated. The King is with us; we cannot be overcome. The King is with us; we cannot be lost. Wherever we go, regardless of the hardships of the journey, as followers of the King we go with joy in our hearts. A seminary professor was teaching a class of preachers. He was telling them how important it is for one's facial expression to be consistent with the substance of the message. He said, "When you are speaking of heaven, let your face light up. Let your face radiate a heavenly gleam. Let your eyes shine with reflected glory. Of course, when you are speaking about hell your ordinary face will do."

My friends, the ordinary face will not do for Christian people. Our faces must reflect the glory of the kingdom of God and the joy that has come to us. The victory has been won! We have been saved! Our sins are forgiven! We look to the future with hope and promise.

Christian people need to reflect in their lives and worship the true victorious nature of faith. Too often we come to worship, offer our prayers, sing magnificent hymns and hear the saving word of God with a look on our faces as if our nearest and dearest died just yesterday. Christian people need to lighten up! Christ is the Victor! We celebrate with our King as members of his royal family. We do not grieve as if we have been banished from his kingdom. Let there be joy in our hearts! Our King is with us!

Teresa Bloomingdale is an author who has a talent for finding something good in everything. In 1975, she and her family went into the cellar for protection against an approaching tornado. The tornado swept across the land and literally blew their house away leaving nothing but the cellar. Fortunately, no one was injured. When Teresa Bloomingdale looked at the scene of devastation she didn't grieve and cry about the terrible loss. Instead, she viewed the twisted rubble for a moment and observed, "We were planning to move in a few weeks, now I don't have to pack all those things." She found the strength for joy even in a tragic moment.

The way of the Christian life is that we don't walk around morbidly with sour, somber faces. We walk the road, even though it is difficult, with joy in our hearts and on our faces. The Shepherd King leads us.

I want to let you in on a truly remarkable discovery. The Shepherd King not only leads us, he needs us. Can you imagine that? God needs you! The Almighty God, who created the universe and put the stars in their places, needs you. There are so many of his children who are hungry, lost, lonely, thirsty and in need. God turns to you for a hand that will reach out, a voice that will encourage and a heart that will care.

Psychologist James Lynch wrote a book about loneliness in which he makes the startling observation that loneliness kills. He says it is our nature, our biological nature, to need human relationships that matter. He suggested that if our need for relationships is not met, our health is literally in peril. He concludes that either we love one another or we die.

Jesus understood our need for someone to care and he said, "Love one another as I have loved you (John 13:34)." In Matthew 25 we find a marvelous passage where the Shepherd King says to the sheep at his right hand, "Come, O blessed of my father, enter into the kingdom that has been prepared for you from the foundation of the world. I was hungry and you fed me. I was thirsty and you gave me drink. I was a stranger and you welcomed me. I was naked and you clothed me. I was sick and you visited me. I was in prison and you came to me. And the righteous asked the Lord, 'When did we see you hungry or thirsty or sick or in prison?' And he answered, 'As you have done it to the least of these my brothers and sisters, you have done it to me' (Matthew 25:34-40)." God needs us to be his hands, his voice, his heart.

One night as a man was walking down the street he was suddenly attacked by a group of thugs. He was beaten, dragged into an alley and left for dead. As he was lying bleeding on the ground, he looked up into the dim amber light in the alley and saw the face of another looking at him. He felt the touch of someone's hands lifting his shoulder. At that moment, he lost consciousness. In the hospital, when he regained consciousness, he remembered the face in the alley and asked, "Is the one who helped me here? I want to speak to him." "Yes," the nurse answered, "He is here and has been waiting to see you." When the man walked into the room, the one who was injured said, "I want to thank you for helping me in the alley this evening and I want to tell you something. When I looked up into that dim light and saw your face, I thought you were Jesus." The man smiled and said, "When I heard your voice calling for help, I thought you were Jesus."

Jesus is in us all. He is in those who need help and those who give it.

There is a wonderful hymn about the Shepherd King. The first stanza reads:

"The King of Love my Shepherd is
whose goodness never faileth.
I nothing lack if I am his
and he is mine forever."

Our King is not a king distant and removed. He is a king here with us today; and we lack nothing if we are his and he is ours forever. To our Shepherd King be all honor and glory, now and forever. Amen.

A Note Concerning Lectionaries And Calendars

The following index will aid the user of this book in matching the correct Sunday with the appropriate text during Pentecost. All texts in this book are from the series for Lesson One, Common Lectionary. Lutheran and Roman Catholic designations indicate days comparable to Sundays on which Common Lectionary Propers are used.

(Fixed dates do not pertain to Lutheran Lectionary)

Fixed Date Lectionaries *Common and Roman Catholic*	Lutheran Lectionary *Lutheran*
The Day of Pentecost	The Day of Pentecost
The Holy Trinity	The Holy Trinity
May 29-June 4 — Proper 4, Ordinary Time 9	Pentecost 2
June 5-11 — Proper 5, Ordinary Time 10	Pentecost 3
June 12-18 — Proper 6, Ordinary Time 11	Pentecost 4
June 19-25 — Proper 7, Ordinary Time 12	Pentecost 5
June 26-July 2 — Proper 8, Ordinary Time 13	Pentecost 6
July 3-9 — Proper 9, Ordinary Time 14	Pentecost 7
July 10-16 — Proper 10, Ordinary Time 15	Pentecost 8
July 17-23 — Proper 11, Ordinary Time 16	Pentecost 9
July 24-30 — Proper 12, Ordinary Time 17	Pentecost 10
July 31-Aug. 6 — Proper 13, Ordinary Time 18	Pentecost 11
Aug. 7-13 — Proper 14, Ordinary Time 19	Pentecost 12
Aug. 14-20 — Proper 15, Ordinary Time 20	Pentecost 13
Aug. 21-27 — Proper 16, Ordinary Time 21	Pentecost 14
Aug. 28-Sept. 3 — Proper 17, Ordinary Time 22	Pentecost 15
Sept. 4-10 — Proper 18, Ordinary Time 23	Pentecost 16
Sept. 11-17 — Proper 19, Ordinary Time 24	Pentecost 17

Sept. 18-24 — Proper 20, Ordinary Time 25	Pentecost 18
Sept. 25-Oct. 1 — Proper 21, Ordinary Time 26	Pentecost 19
Oct. 2-8 — Proper 22, Ordinary Time 27	Pentecost 20
Oct. 9-15 — Proper 23, Ordinary Time 28	Pentecost 21
Oct. 16-22 — Proper 24, Ordinary Time 29	Pentecost 22
Oct. 23-29 — Proper 25, Ordinary Time 30	Pentecost 23
Oct. 30-Nov. 5 — Proper 26, Ordinary Time 31	Pentecost 24
Nov. 6-12 — Proper 27, Ordinary Time 32	Pentecost 25
Nov. 13-19 — Proper 28, Ordinary Time 33	Pentecost 26 Pentecost 27
Nov. 20-26 — Christ the King	Christ the King

Reformation Day (or last Sunday in October) is October 31 (Common, Lutheran)

All Saints' Day (or first Sunday in November) is November 1 (Common, Lutheran, Roman Catholic)